I0436896

From The Ground Up:

A Common Sense Approach to Building a Foundation for High Student Achievement!

Worth Forbes

Bloomington, IN

authorHOUSE·

Milton Keynes, UK

AuthorHouse™
1663 Liberty Drive, Suite 200
Bloomington, IN 47403
www.authorhouse.com
Phone: 1-800-839-8640

AuthorHouse™ UK Ltd.
500 Avebury Boulevard
Central Milton Keynes, MK9 2BE
www.authorhouse.co.uk
Phone: 08001974150

First published by AuthorHouse 4/10/2006

ISBN: 1-4259-2054-3 (sc)

Library of Congress Control Number: 2006901467

*Printed in the United States of America
Bloomington, Indiana*

This book is printed on acid-free paper.

Dedication

This book is dedicated to Granddaddy, Grandmama, and Mama. Thanks for teaching me how to live and enjoy life. You instilled in me the importance of hard work, determination, and trusting God.

Acknowledgements

Much appreciation and thanks to .....

Karen, for bringing joy to our household and for
supporting me in reaching my goals in life.

Thompson, for being the best son
any father could ever have.

Caroline, for being the best daughter
any father could ever have.

Daddy, for your encouragement
in writing this book.

Ted, for years of friendship and support.

Kristy, for your input and suggestions from
a teacher's point of view on this endeavor.

Jeff, for your input and suggestions from an
administrator's point of view on this endeavor.

My friends at Hollywood Grill, who offer
lively antidotes to life's problems and get
my day started with optimism.

Table of Contents

Foreword

America's education system needs major changes if our country desires to be the world leader when it comes to educating our children and young adults. America's high school freshman class, on an average, will not graduate nearly 30% of enrolled students (Ewell, Jones, & Kelly, 2003). We cannot be a leader of this world in economics, science, math, medical, agriculture, and many other fields if we continue with these failing statistics. Researchers Robert Balfanz and Nettie Legters (2004) found that one-half of African-American students and nearly 40 percent of Latino students attend high schools where most of the students did not graduate.

Researchers have also found that many of the students who do graduate from high school are poorly prepared for a job or college. More than 50 percent of high school graduates have to take one or more remedial classes in college (Parsad & Lewis, 2003).

The problems that we are seeing in our high schools did not occur over night. There has been a slow process that has taken place over the last few years, and now we as a nation are just beginning to see the effects of the poor performance of our educational system. Our elementary and middle schools have not stepped up to the plate and prepared our students for high school. The end product - our seniors - tells the story of how our educational system is working. As you can see from the research statistics above, we are not doing a great job of educating our youth.

Many of our students are promoted from one grade to the next grade without a good background in literacy and mathematic skills. The Education Trust Research Group has reported that nearly three-fourths of eighth graders cannot read at a proficient level (The Education Trust, 2003).

This book provides a common sense approach that, if enacted, will improve the educational system for the students who attend school in America. Many of the strategies and techniques that are discussed in this book are common sense strategies, but organized in a way that will help educators and parents identify what might need adjusting in their child's school setting. The ultimate goal is to ensure optimal learning.

Oftentimes, we as educators know what needs to be changed or done to make a school more successful, but don't implement those strategies, because they may not be "politically correct". This book does not take political correctness into account when it comes to student achievement. There is no program that is more important than one which ensures that students get the proper education. You will read about the importance of having a vision, analyzing test data, implementing strategies that improve student learning, and implementing a strong and consistent discipline program.

I have been a principal in three schools in Pitt County, North Carolina. The schools in which I have been the principal have all been very successful. This book explains the strategies that I implemented to change the schools into environments where students begin to reach their potential in the learning process. Change took place, happened quickly, and the community experienced success in the achievement of tomorrow's society.

Following are charts which will show the growth that took place in each of the schools where I was principal. The growth factor is a calculation that shows how much growth the students made in one year. We have several categories in North Carolina that take into account the growth of students. The two highest performing categories are expected growth and high growth. Schools making expected growth attained their expected growth standard as set by the state of North Carolina. In other words, the state said school A should make this amount of growth and, if it does, it receives a title of Expected Growth.

Schools making high growth attained their high growth standard as set by the state of North Carolina. Schools making high growth exceed growth beyond what the state requires for that particular school. As you will see in the following Exhibit A, the three schools where I was principal met or went beyond what the state expected of each every year.

In Exhibit B, you will see a chart showing the performance of each of the schools where I was principal. The performance composite shows the percentage of students in a specific school at or above grade level in a specific school. That percentage increased every year except one, and that year I was promoted to a new position at our system's central office level in mid-school year.

Exhibit A: **Growth Factor**

Year	School	ABC Growth
1998	Pactolus Elementary	High
1999	Chicod School	High
2000	Chicod School	High
2001	Chicod School	High
2002	Chicod School	Expected
2003	Farmville Central High School	High
2004	Farmville Central High School	High
2005	Farmville Central High School	High

Exhibit B: **Performance Composite**

Year	School	Performance
1998	Pactolus Elementary	43.1% to 53.2%
1999	Chicod School	69.4% to 75.4%
2000	Chicod School	75.4% to 82.6%
2001	Chicod School	82.6% to 86.1%
2002	Chicod School	86.1% to 93.0%
2003	Farmville Central High School	71.5% to 74.7%
2004	Farmville Central High School	74.7% to 84.4%
*2005	Farmville Central High School	84.4% to 82.0%

* In January of this year I assumed the responsibilities as the Director of 9-12 of Pitt County Schools, and at the same time, continued as the principal of Farmville Central High School.

As educators, parents and community leaders, we must demand better from our educational system in this nation. All students should be challenged to their potential and given a rigorous course of study, whether in elementary or high school. We are not only molding our future leaders, but also our future parents, future health care workers and every other field that one can imagine.

This book will help parents as well as educators see a "common sense approach" to student performance. As a parent, I would want to read a book that would explain to me in simple language the way a school should operate to ensure that my child receives the best education possible. This book will also help administrators and teachers organize and change teaching strategies, so that the students of America will receive the best education possible. Our objective as an American Educator should be to provide an educational system for all of our children that will be the envy of the rest of the world.

Chapter 1

First Impressions

Plunked down into a school as The New Principal, your task is laid before you: the shortcomings of previous administrators haunting your office, test scores in a nosedive, diva moms vying for your undivided attention, staff with their own agenda, and a campus in need of an extreme makeover. Your job: to whip it into shape. The main focus: everything. What this book is about: bringing it all together into an optimized learning environment that will turn out young adults who are equipped for society. Specifically, we will take a step-by-step trip through the paces of establishing your presence as the leader of your school to the culmination of daily tasks and strategies that will produce a successful and well-equipped crop of graduates.

Working in a school system can be an interesting experience. As administrators, many times we move from school to school. Once we are assigned to our new school and our name hits the newspaper, faculty members, staff, students and parents begin to share all the stories that they know about you as a person and as an educator. At the moment you are assigned to the school, all eyes are on you as a person, administrator and as a professional. When you first visit the school and meet the staff, you are projecting an important message that could impact the amount of success that you have at the school. What you say, how you act, how you present yourself and even down to the eye expressions you make will affect how your staff, parents, students and community view you as a person. You must be in control of your actions and present yourself as a person who really cares for people.

I was principal in a rural school that had enjoyed the same principal for over ten years. The people in this community and the teachers had been accustomed to the same principal for several years, so they all were set in their routines. Prior to my tenure the superintendent replaced this long term principal with a person who was from outside the county. The new principal entered the school without communicating a strong vision and message, and at the same time, made numerous changes. The community did not agree with the changes from the start. I lived in this community and heard many of the conversations that were discussed in the local gathering places. A large part of the changes were being taken negatively. The teachers and the administration were not on the same page, so there were staff members contributing to the negativity surrounding the possible changes that the new principal was implementing. Negative feelings escalated to the point that the community and staff were beginning to question student learning, finances, personnel practices, and even the beautification program for the campus. About three years into this principal's tenure, student learning began to suffer. Focus was placed on examining every move the principal made, as if his or her actions were under a microscope rather than student learning. The principal had many good ideas, and I do not believe he or she did anything ethically or educationally wrong as Principal. But, by not coming into the school without selling a vision, focused on a mission, the principal was doomed from the start. As a result of community unrest and pressure, the principal resigned at the end of his or her third year.

A few days after I heard that this principal was going to leave, I was approached about becoming the new principal at this school. Of course, I accepted the challenge; one that I knew would require much time and energy. I followed specific steps that helped me turn the school into the highest performing school in the county. The steps that I implemented involved the following:

1. Projecting a high profile positive message

2. Communicating a vision specific to the school

3. Being compassionate

4. Being a great listener

5. Promoting the concept that "All Students Can Learn"

By using these strategies, the stage was set for success. Ultimately, this plan proved itself for me and it will work for you. Here are your steps for success:

First impressions are everything.

When meeting staff, greet them warmly and look them straight in the eyes when they are talking to you, being calm yet confident in your look. Communicate, from the very beginning, your vision for the school with parents, students, and faculty members. The vision should be one that sends the message that all students can learn, and nothing less. Deliver the message that as long as you are the administrator of this school, you will give it your best to make this a school environment where all students will learn. You will exhaust all means to ensure student proficiency. You also must allow your compassion to be felt by anyone with whom you speak.

Being compassionate is a very powerful tool that should be a part of your everyday actions. The staff needs to know that you truly care and that you are not putting on some kind of an act. The staff in the school's environment should realize that what they are discussing with you is important. Most anyone can tell when we are talking to someone, if the individual we are talking to is really interested in what we are saying. You can tell by a person's look or the way they are responding if they are truly interested or in tune to what you are saying. Stop what you're doing when a staff member enters your office to talk to you. If you do not, you are showing a definite lack of respect for your staff members. You should convey an image of one who respects others if you want your staff to learn to respect you, the students, and the parents of your community. Be in tuned to the people you talk to at all times, no matter how large or small the problem.

Listening is communication.

Make it your goal to be a great listener. An administrator needs to be a great listener for as long as he/she is the principal, while at the same time being consistent with stating his or her vision/message. As the principal communicates with the staff and parents, a perception of the principal and his ideas is being formed. The perception that the community and staff has of the principal is extremely important. The way they perceive the principal is as important as the actual way he or she really feels. It does not matter if a principal has a great vision for the school if he/she cannot communicate it effectively to the community and staff.

We have a vision.

Create a vision specific to the school that stresses the individuality and high potential of each student in the school. The school's vision should stress a theme, one in which you would want at every school, and that is a theme that challenges each student to his or her top potential. Teachers will play an integral part in selling this vision. Enlist staff input; this will further establish ownership of the vision by the very ones who will be essential to day-to-day promotion of the school's mission.

Parents demand a vision for their child's school which will prepare their child for whatever they do once he or she graduates. This thought or vision must begin in kindergarten and be promoted throughout that child's school career. As a parent, who would want anything less for their children? At this point, some of you may say that there are some parents who could care less about a vision for their child's school or for their own child for that matter, and I agree. But at the same time, we need to operate as if all parents want the best for their child and will do all they can to see to it that their child gets a quality education.

"All."

Promote the concept that "All students can learn." An administrator needs to create an environment where all children can learn. When you think about it, that is what your vision should be. If we accomplish this task, everything else will fall into place, because when you create this type of environment in a school, you are taking care of areas, problems, situations that must be fixed before you reach the type environment where all students can learn. You will have educators who will talk to you about different kinds of theories, and that is good. But state a vision that will get the best out of students, reach for the top, and create an environment where all children can learn.

I look at stating a vision like building a house. When you begin to build a new house, you have already selected your plan. You know the look you want it to have, the design, the color, the size and the type furniture you would like the house to occupy. What are you doing when you are selecting these factors? You are trying to fulfill your vision. This is what I want in a house. I want the best house I can have. This is my top product. To get that new house that you want, you begin to work or have workers start with the foundation and work up, all the time having in your mind your finished product, your vision.

Now, I will be the first to admit that we may start that new house, and as we go along with the construction, we may want to make a few changes, but we still have a vision of what we want to see when the construction is complete. This is the way it is with education. Have a vision: one that all others fall under. Aim for the top idea and begin working from the bottom up making sure you are building a strong foundation. From day one, you must set the stage for an impression that is received from your staff, parents, students and community that anything they come up with will fall under your vision, a vision that is the ultimate, the one that states that all students can learn no matter what their abilities.

Chapter 2

Analyze Data

Your first impressions have been set for the school. In the previous chapter, we discussed how to set a positive impression for your school and how to communicate a vision. While you are forming impressions and promoting your vision, the test data from the school must be analyzed. A vision cannot ignore the reality presented in the data. The vision should embrace the data to enhance results. I can remember being assigned as a principal to a school that was labeled by the state of North Carolina as low performing. The proficiency rate (students scoring at or above level three on state tests) for the students at this school was below fifty percent. Any school scoring below fifty percent as a total school population was considered low performing.

It was hard for the teachers to understand why the proficiency rate of the students was below fifty percent, but it was my job as the newly appointed principal to analyze test data and be as straightforward as I could be with the staff. At the same time, it was my duty to encourage them as much as possible to make productive changes.

It was important to me as the school's instructional leader to be as positive as I could be and motivate the staff to see where they could improve. I would use test data to accomplish the task of getting them to see areas where they could improve.

There were days that I left this school feeling very sad for the staff members. The staff members came to school each day, worked as hard as they could, dealt with irate parents at times, encountered student discipline problems and had to change the way they had been doing things for so many years, yet their school still had the lowest scores in the county. That was tough for a staff to endure.

I wanted to paint a picture for the staff, using their previous years test scores, that would help them shift their emphasis to areas of need. We analyzed the test scores as a total staff, implemented changes, and worked extremely hard as a team. We moved our school in that one year from a school that was labeled by the state as low performing to a school that was exemplary. An exemplary school is one that made more progress toward student performance than the stated expected. It was a great accomplishment for the staff, students, and community. As an instructional leader, it was one of the most rewarding days of my life. I was thrilled to go back to the school after I learned that the hard work had paid off and our school was now going to be recognized by the state of North Carolina as being an "exemplary school."

To help accomplish this recognition, we followed a process that allowed us to analyze test data and see as a team how to improve our teaching strategies and what areas we needed to emphasize.

The following is a simple process to use when studying data:

Test Data Review Process:

1. Gather three years of data

2. Share with various groups in the school and community

3. Analyze the data using charts and graphs

4. Disaggregate the data by race, gender and socioeconomics

5. Identify areas of achievement and areas of needs or concerns

6. Share the results of your analysis with the total staff

It is vital that the principal get all the test data, demographics and climate surveys from his or her school and analyze it with a fine-toothed comb. If possible, get at least three years of data from your school. In the high schools, not only would you look at test scores, but also drop-out rates, graduation rates, advanced placement scores, SAT scores, Career-Technical scores, and any other data you can pull together. The data gathered would differ depending on the grade level of the school and the requirements of each state.

Once you have collected the data, the principal, teachers, community leaders, and student representatives should analyze the data placed in spreadsheets where they can compare scores. You will need to disaggregate the data by race, gender, and socioeconomics. Identify the low achieving areas and look for patterns of low performance, making note of patterns of achievement in certain courses or areas. The patterns help you to identify areas where the school may need to place an emphasis during the school year. Look at how individual teacher's students have performed over a series of years to help identify strengths and weaknesses in staff members. This can help in determining which teachers should teach which subjects each year.

You should analyze data so that it will clearly show the message that you are trying to convey. The test data charts and graphs should show a clear picture so that teachers will be able to understand why you have chosen this area(s) as a focus during the year. It is also important to share broad areas of concern, without identifying teachers or individual students.

Disaggregating data is extremely important in charting your course. Disaggregating data is looking at groups of students and specific objectives to see strengths and weaknesses. When looking at a school's disaggregated data, the school can see where achievement gaps are located and with which groups. A principal should ask himself or herself if all groups—for example, minorities, male/female, and free & reduced lunch, etc.— are achieving at the same rate. If they are not achieving at the same rate, then there is work to be done.

Identify areas of achievement where students are not experiencing growth. When you look at your data, you may see that your lower functioning students are growing at a slower rate than your higher achieving students. If this is the case, then the teachers would need to implement higher-level teaching strategies, strategies that will challenge these students. All students should be experiencing growth from one year to the next in their level of learning. How sad it is for a student to be in a classroom a whole year and not show any growth. You must keep in the forefront of your mind that "all students can learn". All of your decision-making and implementation of learning strategies must be based on this premise.

Continue to review test-specific data that can be analyzed which will steer you in the direction that you need in order to continue moving towards your destination. Specifically you need to observe how students are progressing in reading, writing, and math. These are not the only areas where data should be studied, but areas should be the initial emphasis of the preliminary observation. Another way to observe how students are progressing would be to compare subgroups, such as minorities, exceptional students, race, and gender. Gather the data and place in a bar graph. An example of comparing scores among white and black students would be the following:

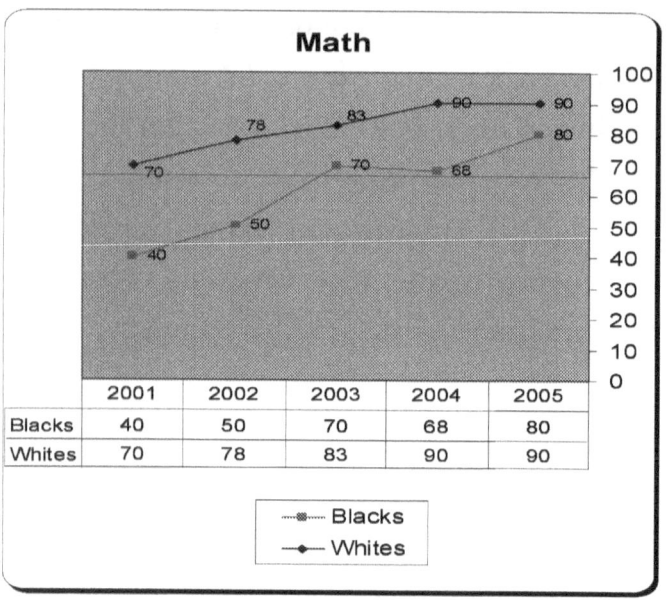

Math

	2001	2002	2003	2004	2005
Blacks	40	50	70	68	80
Whites	70	78	83	90	90

Blacks
Whites

When examining the line graph, you can see that both groups are progressing but there is still a gap. You would graph each subject matter the same, be it elementary or high school. In high school, you may have more subjects to graph. The graph will be determined by which subject the State Board of Education emphasizes, or the subjects you as an administrator would emphasize.

As an administrator/educator, I feel that it is important to analyze all subjects and or areas of study, starting with math, and reading. Math and reading are the basis for all other subjects. Students must be able to read with understanding if they are to achieve and be successful.

Other data to review would be the students' percentage proficient on specific objectives. The teacher should identify specific objectives on which the student is weak so that he or she would be able to alter the instructional process in his/her classroom. Weak objectives must be identified so that the teacher can develop activities that will reinforce the learning process of that specific objective. Hopefully by focusing on weak objectives the students will increase their knowledge base in that particular area of study.

In conclusion, you will find that analyzing data is the map that will direct your course. Analyze, differentiate, graph, diagnose, and study the data. Be sure and have a clear sense of direction for your school, class, or student before you leave the analyzing stage. Our next chapter will cover an invasive plan of action.

Chapter 3

The Plan of Action

Now that you have analyzed data, gathered conclusions, and identified the strengths and weaknesses, you can start constructing a plan of action that will ensure student proficiency. It is not productive to just sit around and discuss data without putting into place a plan of action. The plan of action should address the issues that your data in Chapter 2 identified. Every issue is cause for a specific action. Again, the entire school needs to be constant with our vision, often reminding yourself, your teachers, parents and community that all students can learn.

The first step in a plan of action is for you, the Principal, to study the data analysis. If you are a teacher, study the data analysis gathered from your classroom(s). If you are a parent, analyze abbreviated data from your child's work. Once you have studied the data, you need to brainstorm several plans of action. Write the plans down with several specifics about each one. You will need to list several strategies that will address the needs of your plan. You have an idea of the specific objectives or goals on which you need to concentrate from studying the data; plan to involve and share the goal and objective items with your school improvement team or leadership team at your school. Parents could brainstorm their ideas with a teacher or counselor if they want to suggest strategies or offer insight into patterns. When you are sharing your test data with the total staff at a school, your objective as an instructional leader is to hope that your team members will see the same strengths and weaknesses. It is much better to lead someone when they can see the problem or strength themselves rather than telling them and pulling them along. It is very difficult, if not impossible, for a person to accomplish a task if the leader is pushing or pulling the team members. The members of the team should be right up there with the instructional leader, moving forward as fast as they can with all the strategies possible to use. You must work as a team to be successful. It is important that you present your data analysis in a way that is easy for your listeners to understand and to interpret.

As a core group, the administrator and School Improvement Team members identify strategies that can be implemented. The team will need to list as many strategies as possible to impact the weak areas and the positive areas. Members may begin providing excuses as to the low scores or gaps between the different groups of students. Do not make this your primary focus; instead you must keep the group's eyes on the ultimate goal: student success. Whether you are the principal, a teacher, or a parent, as the leader you must keep the team or individual(s) focused.

There is no way that I can list all the strategies that teachers can use. The strategies that you implement to accomplish your plan of action must be strategies that the teachers understand how to implement and that engage the students in high level learning. Some examples of strategies that could be implemented are as follows:

Pacing Guides

Pacing guides should be kept by all teachers. A pacing guide follows the standard course of study and helps the teacher pace him/herself throughout the year. This prevents the teacher from spending too much time on a specific objective and not getting to other objectives throughout the year that are vital to the success of students. Each pacing guide objective or skill should be dated with a specific date that identifies the specific date the objective or goal was introduced by the teacher. All dates should correspond with the dates in the teachers' lesson plans.

Involve all Departments or Subjects in the Basics

The teaching of reading and writing skills should be taught in all areas. This includes health and physical education as well as music, etc. It is vital to the students that they are exposed to reading and writing skills in all areas of the disciplines.

When you have all disciplines involved in reading and writing, you are constantly reinforcing important skills that will help ensure success and help the school to reach the vision.

Teachers should teach

Teachers should remain in the classroom with the students at all times. Teachers should be out of the classroom only during their planning times or if an emergency arises. Many of you may ask why I have included this strategy. I can't name the times that I have visited schools and seen teachers out in the halls carrying on conversations about issues that could wait until a later time. The instructional time of the student should be protected. Time on task includes teachers. Protecting instructional time should also be an important consideration when administration and teachers are planning such things as assembly programs, sports events that happen during the school day, and any other events that interrupt instructional time. A strong administration will not let such events be planned too often during the school year. These events cut into instructional time in a way that even your most dedicated teachers cannot control. This is a simple strategy, but one that is very important.

Differentiating instruction in the classroom

Some students in the classroom need a review or maybe perform at a slower pace than others. Students who can maintain a fast pace will perform well. These students need to be challenged as all students must be challenged in order to reach their full potential. A teacher must differentiate instruction so that all students will comprehend the subject matter and at the same time, be sure that the objectives and concepts that will be included on the state testing are covered. This is a hard skill for teachers to accomplish, but one that must be implemented in the teacher's instructional presentation.

Maintain High Time on Task

All students should remain on task throughout the teacher's lesson. Students should be sitting up in their desk and paying attention. Teachers can help make this happen by circulating throughout the classroom monitoring student activity.

Students know which teachers never circulate throughout the classroom. This allows students the opportunity to work on something else at their desk or just not pay attention at all. Upon entering the classrooms in a new school, I can easily identify the teachers who have chosen not to circulate within the classroom. Students have their heads on their desks and often have other materials out that do not relate to the specific objective being taught. Optimal learning is not taking place when this occurs in the classroom.

Once you have brainstormed and listed all the strategies you can use to improve both the weaknesses and the strengths, the team members should then share the test data and plan of action with their grade level or departments. If you are a teacher, you can share your findings with a peer or administrator. If you are a parent, you can share your ideas with a teacher or administrator at your child's school.

The above strategies are just a few that need to be implemented in a school if learning is going to take place. You must be serious about what you are doing in a school when it comes to students' learning.

When the total faculty is made aware of the plan of action for the strengths and weaknesses, it is then time to complete a School Improvement Plan that lists your school's goals and strategies. The goals will be developed from the results of the test data analysis. The various departments or grade levels will submit the ideas that were offered by their departments with the entire team and from these ideas a School Improvement Plan is written. Strategies in the plan need to be very specific and have data to support the inclusion of the strategy. The School Improvement Team members write the School Improvement Plan with the input they receive from all faculty members. The School Improvement Plan should include test scores, objectives, and examples of activities. There should be specific methods included to measure growth in identified areas. This plan should include only strategies that improve test scores and address the potential of each student. A plan that only consists of "frills" does nothing to help improve a school.

Every teacher in the school should follow the SIP. The principal should have a process in place to check to make sure that the SIP is being followed by every teacher. It takes all faculty members to accomplish the goal of a school. We now have a developed plan of action. The next chapter will focus on selling The Plan of Action to all the staff and community.

Chapter 4

Selling the Plan

The analysis has been done and areas of weakness and strength have been identified. You have involved the School Improvement Team and listened to their ideas on the identified areas of concern. The recommendations have been recorded and shared with the staff and a plan has been written. Remember, our optimum goal is to pursue the idea that "all students can learn." We cannot, as educators, just settle for the idea that all students can learn, but we must prove that all students can learn. This is something that must be proven if we are to gain credibility as the curriculum leader.

Now, what is the next step? I believe for you to have the success that you need to have with your students; you must sell the plan that has been put in place. It is important that your faculty has the feeling that they have been a part of the strategies that have been developed. Your School Improvement Team has been a big player in the construction of the plan. It is now important that you get as many of the other faculty members as you can on board. A big part in selling the plan is to identify strong teacher leaders within your school. Meet with your teacher leaders as individuals and discuss in detail the main goals and objectives of the improvement plan. It is not only important that you believe in what you are doing for your school and that the School Improvement Team believes; everyone has to share that confidence. The faculty members should feel that what they are doing is in the best interest of all students. The faculty must not only talk the talk, but walk the walk when it comes to what you are trying to accomplish. A major task that you as an institutional leader must make sure you achieve is the task of selling the plan. What are statements that you may make during the discussion with individual teachers? One main question that you must satisfy with the teacher leaders as well as the general staff is the reason why you have chosen this direction. You must express to them in a broad manner what goals can be reached as a result of this action. Give them a glimpse of what will be the end result.

You need to stress to specific lead teachers that it is their duty to emphasize the positives of the plan. They need to share their positive feelings toward the plan with their peers and community folks that they may see during the week. These folks will be very influential in helping spread the improvement plan.

I look at the key teacher leaders as spokesmen for the plan. Their goal should be to campaign for the plan developed for the school. At times, these individuals may encounter teacher/peers who are not willing to change. It is then their duty as leaders to present the material in a way that will at least enable the reluctant teachers to accept the plan even if they do not embrace it. The Principal as the instructional leader must keep in mind that, for teachers, community leaders and other parties of the school environment to stay on board and support the strategies, the plan must produce positive results.

I can remember a teacher that I worked with at one school who was very hesitant to make changes in her instructional delivery. She was a seasoned teacher who had taught for many years and did not want to change in any way. She did not want to be a part of a new plan for her school. She had worked with several principals and was tired of administrators coming in and making changes that did not produce improved tests results. I felt that I must get this teacher on board, if I was to be successful with many of the other staff members in getting them to make changes in their way of teaching.

It was a hot August day, school had been in session for two weeks, it was time to have a meeting. I was waiting for this teacher to come to my office during her planning period. What was I going to say to get her to join our team in implementing our new plan for this school? She and I had a frank discussion on instructional strategies and how they should be implemented. I listened to her explain reasons for why she did things a certain way. She expressed her concerns to me about change. This teacher stressed to me how hard she worked, and believe me, she worked extremely hard. I commended her on her dedication and hard work, but I stressed to her that it was not always how hard one worked, but how smart one worked.

I discussed with her different teaching strategies and how they impact student success. We had several meetings over a six-week grading period. At each meeting I would commend her on positive things that took place in her classroom, but at the same time give her suggestions of small, yet important changes.

This teacher finally gave her support to the instructional changes that we implemented at this school. But you see, I did not give up on getting her to do what I felt was best for the students. When it comes to student progress, you can never give up on getting staff members to work as a team. You need every player to be part of the "new plan of action" that involves new teaching strategies.

As a new principal of a school, how do you begin by getting teachers on board that have been instructing students a certain way for years? It is a difficult process, but as I have said before, you must master it if you want a successful school with high student performance for all students.

Some teachers may already include some of the proposed strategies in their classrooms; some strategies may be totally new for the teachers, others may be the same strategies that have been used in the past with a few modifications. The important thing to remember is that the plan allows everyone access to all the strategies and a method to implement them effectively. With new strategies, teachers are going to need the training necessary for them to feel good about implementing new techniques and strategies in their classes. This will require staff development for the staff.

Many teachers as well as administrators have a negative connotation with regards to staff development. The staff development presented should directly impact instructional delivery changes by the teacher.

Many of the instructional strategies will include the following: Identifying similarities and differences, homework practices, cooperative learning, setting objective and getting feedback, high level questions, and graphic organizers. Many of the above strategies are reviewed in a book titled <u>Classroom Instruction That Works</u>, by Robert J. Maguire, Debra J. Pickering and Jane E. Pollock. This is a great resource for your staff. Staff development is very important to the success of your improvement plan. It must be concise, purposeful and point toward positive results.

Another strategy that the principal as well as staff can do to help sell the plan is to accept as many speaking engagements as possible to summarize and promote your plan of action. Speak specifically about what your school will do to help close the achievement gap, improve test scores for all groups of students, for example: minorities, Hispanics, high performing students, low performing students.

It is important that your plan of action has something in it for all the populations that attend your school. There must be strategies that will improve performance of minorities, high as well as low performing students, and also your average students. Parents must feel that there is something in the school's plan for their children. When parents feel that you are implementing strategies that will help their children, they are going to feel good about what changes are taking place. That will enlist their support and encouragement of the school objectives which will positively influence their children.

Now that you have your plan sold, then it is up to you to monitor the strategies that have been put in place. The next chapter will focus on monitoring the plan of action which will enhance student learning.

Chapter 5

Monitoring the Plan

Much time has been spent analyzing, meeting, organizing, presenting and communicating with publics regarding the school's plan of action. The action plan has been decided upon with much input from various sources. It is imperative now that all the goals and strategies are implemented. The Principal, as an instructional leader, must monitor the implementation of the plan.

How can a principal monitor the implementation process with so many demands placed upon his/ her shoulders? Also, if teachers are implementing new strategies in their classroom, how can they monitor themselves? How can parents make sure their child is being challenged?

First, let's examine how the administration will monitor. This is the most important job of an administrator as an instructional leader. It is essential that the Principal personally monitor how instruction is taking place in the classrooms. The administrator must set a personal goal for him/her to visit the classrooms on a weekly basis. That is: *every* classroom in the building. Every classroom includes Physical Education to Advanced Placement English.

Very few weeks passed by during the school year that I did not visit each classroom. Classrooms may be visited on the same day, or visits may be spread over a number of days. As you circulate through the classroom, make notes pertinent to what is observed taking place. I call the weekly visit a "walk through" because I only stayed from two to five minutes in each classroom, longer if needed. During this time, make mental notes, or anecdotal notes, regarding what you see in the class. Observe what strategies the teacher use to promote learning. Look for high student time-on-task, teacher circulation, student engagement in an activity if one was taking place at the time;

and student attention. You do not want to see any students with their heads on the desks, unless they are sick. At all times, look to see that students are engaged in activities that stretch their thinking skills. Teachers should be asking high level questions that challenge all levels of students.

From an administrative viewpoint, a classroom practice that I discouraged was note taking and copying notes from the overhead. To me, too much note taking is a waste of time. Teachers were instructed to make copies of notes and outlines and give them to the students. This allowed the teacher to use the time that students would be taking notes to actively engage them in activities which cover the strategies set in the plan of action. The only way an administrator will know if this is taking place is to be in the classrooms.

Three weeks before major testing, I visited classrooms twice per week to monitor strategies. One week before major testing—for example, End of Course Testing, Achievement Testing, or End of Grade Testing—I would visit the classroom daily. Whenever I visited a classroom and strategies that we had set forth as a school were not being covered, I made contact with the teacher to get an explanation of why the strategies were not in place. I would quickly get the teacher back on track. Many times I would have teachers observe veteran teachers or teachers who were implementing strategies that promoted high level learning. At this point in time, after the plan has been devised, there is no option as to whether or not a teacher should incorporate the strategies in the plan.

My goal to visit all classrooms frequently was met with criticism by colleagues and some administrators from other districts. Criticisms included having my fingers in the teaching process too much. "How do you visit all classrooms to that degree and get the rest of your administrative work accomplished?" Upper level managers would take a "wait and see" attitude, fearing micromanagement themselves of my tactics. Colleagues would say I pushed too hard, while, at the same time, keeping an eye peeled on my work, just waiting to see results. Teachers, on the other hand would complain that my methods kept them on pins and needles, never knowing what to expect. Eventually, teachers grew to appreciate that their work- their craft- was finally being seen by higher ups. Otherwise, the only ones in judgment of their expertise were the ones whom they were teaching. Teachers became more prepared, energetic and proud.

As for it being an addition to my workday, I ask, what is my purpose for being here? Could all other administrative duties fall to second place for the sake of student excellence? This is a topic reserved specifically for an entirely different book on the purposes of school administrators. Stay tuned. My charge to you for now is: Just what is my purpose as an administrator?

At one school where I was Principal, I was met with much resistance when it came to monitoring the instructional process. The teachers felt intimidated when I visited their classrooms. Many teachers had never been visited on a regular basis by their past administrators. As a result, the teachers would gather at lunch, sharing what was happening in their classrooms when I visited. Some would say that "Mr. Forbes didn't come in my room today, so I must be on the right track". Others would make the comment that the reason Mr. Forbes visited their classroom was because they were not on the right track, and that they must be doing something instructionally wrong.

As days went by, the teachers found out that I would continue to visit classrooms on a weekly basis, often giving them feedback on what I observed. Many of the teachers started to appreciate my visits. They began to see that I was interested in what was taking place in their classrooms.

At times, teachers would stop by my office after school and ask how they did when I visited their classrooms that particular day. Most of the time, I would give them positive feedback. If needed, I would also let them know when I saw a need for improvement. It was important to be honest with the teacher. My ultimate goal was high student performance, and to reach that goal, it took this type of monitoring to hone the teacher's instructional skills.

Another way I monitored the plan of action was through the teacher's lesson plans. The teachers would turn in their lesson plans to the administrator on a weekly basis. Lesson plans had to be complete, concise, and fully outline aspects of the next week's lessons. Specifically, teachers had to use the Standard Course of Study to develop the lesson plans.

In preparation of lesson plans, teachers should concentrate on the specific objectives that need to be learned by the students for them to be successful in the subject matter. Teachers should place great emphasis on the objectives or goals that are stressed in the tested areas of the subject matter. Again, the teachers' lesson plans must be based on the standard course of study objectives. All lesson plans should include the following:

1. Objective – The objective should be labeled with the specific number   that is corresponds with in the standard course of study.

2. Source – The source will include the text, page number or where the information was located.

3. Include an activity. Activities should be stated using the following vocabulary words: analyzing, inferring, evaluating, formulating, describing, supporting, explaining, summarizing, comparing, contrasting, tracing, and graphing, and any other words that enlist high level thinking skills on the part of the student(s).

4. Assessment – This is the closure of the lesson. This may be an oral quiz or a game. This part of the lesson plan helps the teacher identify whether he/she has accomplished the objective(s) of the lesson.

I always checked lesson plans every Thursday after school. Each lesson plan would be checked for that week and initialed with a comment. I would return the lesson plans back to the teachers' mailboxes before they returned to school on Friday.

In addition to the walk through strategy and lesson plans, an entire period observation is also used by developing a long range schedule. Teachers are informed that there will be two unannounced observations and one or two announced observations. It is also important that you set up an observation schedule where you will observe teachers for the entire lesson. Many of these observations will be unannounced. You will observe the lesson and give written feedback. Many of the Local Education Agencies have specific plans or procedures that set the standards for classroom observation.

I have known administrators to get distracted by discipline issues, paper work, budget issues or parent concerns and not observe teachers regularly. Teachers must be observed, given both positive and constructive feedback as needed. Poor or mediocre teachers must be placed on an action plan. If their poor performance does not improve, then it is your duty to get them out of your school. This action will take much documentation, but it is an action that must be taken. I always went by the following statement,

"If I didn't want my own kids to have a specific teacher, then I didn't want anyone else's child to have the teacher." He or she either improves or they have to go. Almost always, if you as an administrator give the teacher the support he or she needs you would see improvement. Teachers generally want to do the best job possible. As an administrator, I gave them all the support that was possible. When the teachers feel their administrator is striving for the best, the teachers will follow his lead. Again, it's important that you "lead" staff members toward improvement by positive suggestions and examples you may demonstrate yourself. This is more effective than "pushing" them.

Now, we will change courses and discuss discipline. You can have the best school improvement plan in the world, but if the school does not have good discipline, all is for naught.

Chapter 6

Discipline

Discipline is an issue that can make the difference in a teacher's and school's success. I truly believe that most teachers who leave the field of education do so due to discipline issues. I believe that the biggest roadblock to student drop-out is not lack of money or lack of qualified staff but the issue of discipline. Lack of discipline in our schools is the issue that is keeping many of our students from learning. You can have one student in a classroom who constantly causes disruption and this one student can hinder the learning process for all students. Most teachers try modifications, classroom discipline strategies, making contact with parents and even sending the student to the principal's office for disciplinary action, and still have to deal with the same issues from the student over and over throughout the year. This is very frustrating to a teacher and it is also very frustrating to the students who want to learn. For the most part, students want to learn and they get tired of a particular student constantly disrupting the class.

There comes a time when an administrator has to make a choice – Do I allow the student to stay in school and disrupt the classroom, or do I suspend this student? I am probably suggesting an unpopular position, but when it comes to a classroom of students trying to learn and one or two students constantly disrupt in the classroom, those students will be dealt with in a manner that removes him/her from the classroom to allow the other students to learn. I am not saying that the administration should throw this student out of school and not offer help or services to help correct the behavior. But as an administrator, I drew a line in the sand. If you were a student in the school where I was the principal, you would quickly find out that I set a high standard when it came to learning. If a student attended the school and their main objective was to get attention by disruptive behavior, then you quickly found out that it would not be tolerated. As many educators and philosophers state, "All students can learn," I also believed that "all students can behave in a proper manner where learning can take place." The student chooses not to behave.

Establish a discipline plan early. Let students be aware of the discipline plan from the start of the year and see it in action. As they observe its implementation when their peers are dealt with, they'll know what to expect when they are faced with similar situations. Knowing how they will be disciplined is a key issue in building a student body that respects the rules of their school.

Sometimes I think that as parents and educators, we spend more time trying to make excuses for students rather than trying to address specific problems or situations that are attributing to the disruptive behavior. We say that he/she comes from a broken home, or they are from a low socio-economic family, or their parents don't care about them and so on. We are doing the disruptive student a disservice if we allow them to get away with classroom disruption. Society will not tolerate this in the work place. From kindergarten to grade twelve, we should be preparing all students to be productive and successful citizens, ones that know that certain rules will have to be followed throughout their lives. I look at even the minor things that contribute to not following the rules, such as being tardy for class. There needs to be a consequence for this behavior, not brush it under the rug and ignore it. Think about this: how many employers are going to allow an employee to constantly come in late? Will they allow it over and over again? I think not! If we as educators don't enforce being on time, then we are training a bunch of employees that feel that it is okay to go to work late. The rules and procedures that are taught to students will affect what type of citizens they will become later in life.

Maintaining good discipline involves identifying problem areas early, implementing a discipline policy that supports your state and local polices. It should be a policy that is easy for students, teachers, parents, and the community to understand.

Anyone who has ever worked in a school knows that the administration can make it a wonderful, rewarding experience, or they can make it a daily place of misery. I have had the opportunity to work under eight different head administrators during my days in the classroom. I must say, some of them were most helpful, and others might as well of not ever set foot on campus. In all of my years, I can truly say that I had one who should be the model for every person even considering a job as a school principal.

What made this person such a good leader, you might ask. I can sum this up in a few simple words: support, caring, knowledge of duties, firmness, and fairness. These are qualities that I have found to some degree in many administrators, but to the greatest degree in the one that outshone all of the others I have ever worked under as a teacher.

Support like no other. This man was always there for me as a new teacher. He offered ideas for classroom discipline, parent contacts, and even gave me his opinion on how to handle matters in my personal life. It wasn't that he was trying to be "nosey". He just truly cared about his staff, and we all new it. I have often said that if this man were to ask me to jump off a cliff, I'd say to him, "Tell me where you want me to land?" He had this affect on all of his staff members. His caring nature made us all want to do the best job we could, because we all wanted to please him. We all know that as students, we tried our hardest and did our best work for teachers whom we respected and looked up to. Well, for teachers, it's the same with administrators. When your principal treats you professionally and shows a genuine concern for you as an individual, there are no limits to how hard you will be willing to work for him/her within your school. The same is true of the students within a school. This principal had such a good rapport with the students at our school; he very rarely had any discipline problems to handle. The boys and girls looked up to him and loved him just like his staff, and none of them wanted to do anything to let him down.

I remember once, when I was in my second year at his school, I came into the office one morning early to sign in for the day. I was feeling a little down because I had been having some problems with one particular student in my class. Mr. Jones (as I'll refer to him) met me at the office counter that morning and asked me if something was bothering me. I explained to him that I was having a hard time getting this student to behave in class and I was not sure what to do next. Instead of giving me some long spell about things I should try or instead of questioning my tactics in the classroom, he called me into his office and closed the door behind us. He asked me to sit down in front of his desk and tell him what my concerns were with this student. After I gave my side of the saga, Mr. Jones picked up his phone, without hesitation, and called this boy's mother. When she answered, he calmly, but at the same time sternly said to her, "Ms. G., this is Mr. Jones., principal at your son's school. I am calling to tell you that he has not been behaving the way he should in Mr. Forbes' class the last few days. Mr. Forbes is one of my best teachers and is doing the best job he can teaching your son and helping him control his behavior. I want you to know that this behavior must stop today.....and I do not expect to have to call you about him again. Do we understand each other?....Thank you." And then he hung up, looked over at me, and said, "I don't think you'll have any more problems with him." And he was right.

This principal had a thorough knowledge of the curriculum areas that were to be taught in the grade levels at his school. He was very aware, by drop-in observations, of which teachers were covering the curriculum concepts they needed to cover for his school to be successful. If I thought it would benefit the students at his school to move teachers around to subject areas where they were better suited, he never hesitated to do so. And what may be surprising is that he was very rarely faced with opposition from staff members when he did move them from subjects or grade levels that they were accustomed to, to new areas for instruction. This was because he always knew how to "sell his ideas" for the move in such a way as to not make the teacher feel like it was because he was not satisfied with them as a team member within his school.

Mr. Jones was always fair with all staff members. He didn't play favorites. If you needed correcting, he was there to do it. But at the same time, he never held grudges either. I remember once when I had made the mistake of letting a student get off a bus that was going to be late leaving campus one day due to engine trouble. This student had said that he could walk home, rather than wait for the bus to be fixed. Being new in the teaching profession and rather green at some of the "do's and don'ts" of the job, I let this boy get off the bus and walk to his nearby house. Bad idea! Next morning, first thing, Mr. Jones. showed up at my classroom door with a very unhappy look on his usually kind face. He informed me that the parents of this student had called him after school the previous afternoon and were upset that I had let the boy off the bus, allowing him to walk home. He gave me a rather stern talk about how I was putting him, myself, and the school system in jeopardy when I allowed this student to get off the bus without parental permission. I apologized, shook a little in my shoes, and felt just awful that this person, whom I admired so much, had just "come down on me" in this way.

He explained that it was never to happen again. I promised that it wouldn't. All day that day, in the back of my mind, I was so worried because I had let my boss down. As I said earlier, he was the kind of man that everyone always wanted to please. When I went in the office to sign out that afternoon, I ran right into him again! He asked me how my day had gone. I couldn't help but say, "Well, it went fine except I've worried all day today about what we talked about this morning and about how upset you seemed with me." This is when I really realized what a great leader he was and how fortunate I was to be apart of the school he led. He put his arm around my shoulder and pulled my up to his side and said, "Listen, don't you worry about that one more minute. It was just something we had to get straight, and I have not thought about it another time today. Don't give it another thought, and neither will I. I know you're a great teacher and I'm lucky to have you as a part of my staff." It was amazing how much his words did to lift the heavy burden of worry I had felt all day that day. I knew right then and there, that if I were ever a principal, this would be the man I'd most want to model myself after.

I remember him saying to me at times, that as a teacher and as an administrator, you must have a good discipline plan for your classroom or school. Based upon my experience with Mr. Jones, I can say that I have based much of what I implemented as a principal on what I experienced with Mr. Jones as my principal.

A discipline plan may differ on specific components, from school to school depending on the discipline problems that schools may encounter. But, all plans can have some basic similarities.

The main point regarding a discipline plan is that it should be simple but address issues that come up at the schools. My plan consisted of specific consequences for the students each time they were sent to the office for a disciplinary reason.

At the beginning of the year, it is important that you stress to the teachers that they need to handle as many of their discipline issues as possible. Students will respect them more if they handle discipline issue in their classroom. I always suggested to teachers that they have discipline policies or procedures in place in their classrooms. They need to implement procedures, such as communicating with parents, changing seating arrangements, using positive reinforcement, having a caring attitude, and being consistent with the students when enforcing consequences. Again, if at all possible, the discipline should be handled in the classroom by the teacher. The teacher will be respected much more by the students if he or she handles his or her own discipline in the classroom without involving the administration. This action will make things much better for the teacher if this can take place. The goal of the teacher is to gain respect but at the same time be teaching the student self-discipline. It is important that the teacher implements strategies that make their classroom instruction interesting. If lessons are not interesting, students will naturally become bored and frustrated. This is a sure-fire cause of many minor discipline problems in the classrooms that if left uncorrected, can escalate to more serious problems. I have discussed these strategies and techniques in previous chapters. But, there does come a time when a student will not adhere to whatever the teacher is trying to enforce. At this point, when the teacher has documented all the strategies that he/she has used to try and get this student or students to adhere to classroom policies, then it is the duty of the administration to step in and help the teacher with the student(s). The student must be dealt with by the school administration. Often times, what takes place at this point is the student is talked with by the administration and sent back to class only to return to his/her old habits.

As a principal, if my teachers had tried several strategies, including contacting the parent, and could document the efforts, I supported my teacher with some type of action. My plan was as follows—it is very simple.

1) On the first visit to the office, the student was counseled with and contact made with the parent. This should be a serious conversation with the student and the child's parent.

2) On the student's second visit to the office, he/she was placed in some type of in-school suspension room for one day.

3) On the third referral to the office, the student was assigned for two days in the In School Suspension (ISS) room. Keep in mind that in the ISS room there was an adult monitor assigned that helped students with classroom work missed while in in-school suspension.

Teachers would turn in class work to the ISS program. This time was used to do classroom work. If this rule was broken, they were immediately sent home or, if possible, to where the child's parents were employed. Again, students must be serious about learning and not tolerating misbehavior; this was a part of the philosophy.

4) On the fourth visit to the office, the student was assigned to ISS for three days. This would be the student's last assignment to ISS. After this point, the student would be suspended from school. The parents would be notified of the action. Parents would be called and notified that on the next office referral the student would be suspended from school, beginning with one day. The next time the

student had an office referral, he/she would get an additional day up to ten days. At that point, I would look at long term suspension.

Even though this plan seems cut and dry, which it is, I still am providing the student that is disruptive as much help as I can. This discipline procedure leaves no questions in the minds of the students, teachers, or the parents as to how discipline matters will be handled. I refer the disruptive student to the school's guidance counselor, social worker or any other agency that exists to help troubled, at-risk students who are repeat offenders. These students must not be ignored. We as educators must do all we can to get the misbehaving students on the right track and not be a dropout statistic.

I always operated on four principles when it came to enforcing a discipline policy. They are:

1) Make sure the discipline policy is fair.

2) Enforce the discipline policy consistently.

3) Ask the question: Would I want my own child to follow the rules and regulations I implemented, and

4) Never dismiss the student without offering some kind of help from the school or another agency. The agency needs to try to help modify the student's behavior.

In closing, a school without a good disciplinarian or discipline program that is not consistently enforced will be a school that will fail, no matter how much money is put into educational strategies or programs. Good discipline is a must, if you want to have a successful school, a school where optimal learning takes place.

Chapter 7

Are You Really Serious?

To begin with, it is an honor to be an educator in a school. It is great to be able to celebrate with the faculty, community, and students the success as a school in student achievement. It is a way of life for those of us who work in the schools and put long hours in to our daily adventures to ensure instruction to our students in at an optimum level. When I think of the first day when I became an administrator of a school in my local county, I remember walking in the new school that I was assigned, no one else in the building because it was about 9:30 p.m. at night, I had a flashback of my first day of school as a student. This was the first day that I remember, that I was separated from my family and in unfamiliar territory. I remember the motherly type of atmosphere that the teachers portrayed. My first grade teacher, Ms. Wilma Smith, was an individual who possessed qualities a school administrator would love to have every teacher possesses. She expressed the feelings of caring, being helpful, always picking you up when you felt knocked down. Now think about it, when you think of a school, what comes to mind? I will tell you what comes to mind for most of us, the love, caring and helpfulness that the people in the school taught us. Our schools are more than buildings, it is the people who have worked there, sweated in the halls and rooms, from the custodians to the principal.

When you hear the name of a school mentioned, I bet you start thinking about the school you once attended, remembering….. the times you walked in the front door, down the hall to a classroom, took your seat and waited for class to start. You remember, as a student the times that your parents had argued the night before and you couldn't wait to get to your teacher and share your feelings, knowing that your teacher would say the right words to make you feel better. Remembering…… the times you went outside at recess to play hide and seek or a game of kick ball with your friends. I remember the love letters that I sent to certain girls. I would write in the letter, do you love me, answer yes or no. Most of the time, I got no for an answer. But when I did get a yes, it took away all the pain that I may have felt that day.

When you think about the name of your school, images of people begin to appear in your mind and the influences that they have had upon your life. When I hear my elementary school, Chicod School located in Pitt County, North Carolina, I think of, Mr. Kelly Wallace, Mr. Charles Johnson, both principals, Ms Juanita Elks, 2nd grade teacher, Ms. Frances Porter, Ms. Ina Venters, Ms. Betty LeRoux and I could name many more teachers. What I have become, and what many of you have become, we can truly say our teachers at our schools, had a major part in shaping our lives. The schools we attended become a part of us and that part of us will live in us forever.

Hopefully your local schools have been a unifying presence in the community in which you live or work. It has established families in the community of different backgrounds and races. It has established many friendships.

There will never be a good-bye to the school that you work in as an educator, as either a teacher or principal. The building may one day come down or change, but always remember, the building may be taken from us, but the good memories that we have, the bonds that a wonderful school experience has produced, will be entrenched in our hearts forever.

We will always be able to revisit our schools in our hearts and in our dreams. No matter where we live, the uniqueness of working in a school, with its teachers, cafeteria workers, teacher assistants, custodians, office staff, administration, bus drivers, student, parents, and volunteers will live with you until you depart this Earth, until we leave this world and move to a much greater place in heaven. But you know, I think we all are a little bit better, because we have been part of a school that has been a part of us. May the memories live in our hearts forever.

Many researchers will read this book and state that these strategies have been in place for years, and I agree with that statement. But just because they have existed doesn't mean they are being implemented and monitored. This book helps bring the awareness to the surface of how important the simple things are in an improvement plan for a school. I know that what I have described in this book will work, because I have the improved test/achievement scores to prove the point. In each case I implemented strategies that I have described in this book and in each case the school had increased student achievement.

We spend so much time in education thinking up new ideas and strategies to implement. Often these new strategies are no better than what has been implemented in the past. Oftentimes the strategies are not as productive. I see school systems jump on the band wagon of new ideas. They spend thousands of dollars only to receive mediocre improvements in student achievement. After a few years the school or school system discontinues the program and then jump on another band wagon. We as educators have got to stop jumping from band wagon to band wagon. We must focus on what we have in place, ensure uninterrupted instructional time for all our teachers, support our teachers with necessary materials and supplies, monitor teacher performance and enforce a strict and fair discipline policy.

Teachers are bombarded with new grants or initiatives that take precious instructional time away from the students. Yes, the school district or school gets good publicity from receiving the grant or starting a new program. I have seen grants written that award thousands of dollars but put so much more work and restrictions on teachers that make it not worth the funds awarded. Administrators and teachers need to apply for grants and initiatives that do not tie the hands of our teachers when it comes to instructional delivery.

There are hundreds of so called educational professionals who have been traveling around the world marketing new initiative and programs that do not work. Many schools and school districts struggling with student achievement buy in to these expensive programs, spending thousands of dollars in staff development, staffing needs, materials and supplies. The new program is implemented and the system sees little or no results.

A school system can implement the strategies that I have described with small amounts of new money and see great results. The best investment we have is a strong plan of action and people equipped to implement and exercise the plan. If each component of the plan that I have described in this book is truly implemented, then the school will see great success. I can only imagine the money that could have been spent on reducing class size and building new school facilities for our students and dream about the success of all our students. It sounds simple doesn't it, simple but true. Schools where I have been the administrator have made much improvement in student outcomes.

In conclusion, improving our schools will take more than money, more than thinking up new ideas, or more than jumping on a new bandwagon, but instead a steadfast, knowledgeable team of folks who are willing to implement simple ideas that work rather that what looks or sounds good.

To principals: Evaluate your priorities, making sure that classroom instruction and discovery is the main objective for the day. Support your teachers with positive feed back, help if they need it, and give them freedom to teach!

To teachers: Make it your goal to lead your students to educated success. Seek ways to help students learn, expect them to be the best, and do not allow one person's disruption to negatively impact what is best for all.

To parents: Realize that the team at your child's school has prepared and has been trained to guide your child to academic success. Choose to work hard to help by providing good praise and support of your child's instruction that they received during the school day. Let your child know that doing well in school has its rewards. If your child's teacher contacts you with concerns, join with his or her teacher to get rid of the problem rather than making excuses.

Wake up America! The rest of the world is leaving us behind educationally. Are we as administrators, teachers, parents, and students going to sit back and let this happen? We need to rise up and demand that our schools implement what has been stated in this book before we run off in a new direction. Start from the ground up; let teachers teach. They can't teach with disruptive students in the classroom, they can't teach with their hands tied behind their backs due to implementation of new programs, and they can't teach if we don't leave them alone and let them do their jobs. **Wake up educators, before it's too late!**

References

Balfanz, R., & Legters, N. (2004), *Locating the Dropout Crisis*, Baltimore, MD: Center for Social Organization of Schools.

Education Trust. (2003). *African American Achievement in America*. Washington, DC: Author. Retrieved January 2, 2006, from http://www2.edtrust.org/NR/rdonlyres/9AB4AC88-7301-43FF-81A3-EB94807B917F/0/AfAmer_Achievement.pdf

Ewell, P., Jones, D., & Kelly, P. (2003) Conceptualizing and Researching the Education Pipeline. Boulder, Co: National Center for Higher Education Management Systems.

Parsad, B., & Kelly, P. (2003). Remedial Education at Degree-Granting Postsecondary Institutuions in Fall 2000. Washington, DC: US Department of Education, National Center for Education Statistics. Retrieved January 1, 2006, from http//nces.ed.gov/pubsearch/pubsinfo.asp?pubid=2004010